Waldman House Press, Inc.
525 North Third Street
Minneapolis, Minnesota 55401

THE MARK
OF THE MAKER

Written by Tom Hegg
Illustrated by Warren Hanson

Waldman House Press

This book is dedicated to my father and my son.
T.H.

And to all fathers, and to all sons.
W.H.

"… an angel of the Lord appeared to him in a dream …"

Matthew 2:20

Joseph had only a dream to go on … that and the strength of his character. He had to operate on faith and trust. Those are powerful lessons, though … and ones that must be learned over time.

He must have had a good teacher.

Faithfully,

T.H.

Joseph, this isn't your best work, is it?

oseph?”

“Yes, Papa?”

“Joseph, this isn't your best work, is it?”

Listen carefully. This is Jacob, the Master Carpenter, speaking to his fourteen-year-old son. **“I'm afraid you'll have to do it over — again.”**

Over again! Over again! How many times had Joseph heard his father say those words? This was only the second year of his apprenticeship, but sometimes Joseph felt as if it had already been a lifetime. **“I know I'm not supposed to question your judgment, Papa,”** said Joseph (allowing a slight bit of irritation to season his words), **“but can I ask one question?”**

“May I ask one question.”

“MAY I ask one question?”

“May I ask one question — please.”

“May I ask one question, PLEASE?”

“Of course. Who's stopping you? Ask.”

“Thank you, Papa. Papa, why do I have to do it over

again when it's only a cross-piece for a goat pen?"

"Because the bevel is uneven."

"But Papa, what do the goats care?"

"We'll probably never know. I haven't had a decent conversation with a goat yet."

"Papa ..."

"Yes, Joseph?"

"Papa, please answer me seriously. Papa, why do we always spend so much time on things that people will never even see, Papa? Papa, animals don't really care if a bevel is even, do they? Papa? Papa, are you sure the first one isn't good enough? Papa?"

"So — this is the one question you wanted to ask. Joseph, I've been thinking it over, and you know what? You're absolutely right."

"I am, Papa?"

"Yes. You're NOT supposed to question my judgment. Now do it over again, and this time, mind the grain of the wood the way you were taught."

"But Papa — "

"'But Papa' nothing. Now."

"Yes, Papa."

A fresh puff of delicately sweetened spring air sighed through the shop. It seemed to mock Joseph, hard at his labor. In his mind's eye, he could see himself romping and tumbling with his friends on the flowered hills of Galilee. Could that really have been just two short years ago? And now, long before they were ready, they were men. Well, assistant men, anyway.

Here he was, working with his father ... and Ezra was working for his father, the Miller, and Judah was working for his father, the Cobbler, and his very best friend, Shem, was working for his father, the Goldsmith. Oh! He got a chill whenever he thought of what poor Shem had to go through. Jacob the Carpenter was demanding, yes, but fair and above all a loving father. Ruben the Goldsmith was a high-strung perfectionist given to public displays of temperament and authoritarian tantrums. He had little patience with his inexperienced son.

To make matters worse, Shem had been very small, thin and weak since birth, and it was his further misfortune to have been given poor eyesight. As the only child of Ruben, however, he had to carry the full weight of his father's mighty dreams and ambitions squarely on his frail shoulders.

Just then, Ruben's voice stridently split the air of the shop street. Joseph knew that Shem's poor shoulders were rising yet another permanent notch closer to his ears. At first, Jacob scowled at the sound, but then said, forgivingly, ***"Well, with gold maybe you can be perfect. With wood, I don't know."*** Joseph knew an opportunity when he heard one. ***"Then Papa,"*** he piped up, ***"why am I doing this over again? It'll never be perfect anyway. You said so yourself."***

"Perfect, probably not. But better, of course. Now, work."

In spite of himself, Joseph soon got lost in the enjoyment of his task. Complain though he did from time to time, there was no question that he was well-suited to the carpenter's craft. He was very talented — if a little lazy — and was already developing the powerful, callused and outsized hands of a tradesman.

The wood seemed to obey him at times (the way it always did his father), and he loved to breathe in the moist, pitchy humors of sap and resin from the fresh timber he and Jacob harvested. He was able to pick, by instinct, the finest lengths of raw lumber on those exciting twice-a-year trips to the seaport when his father carefully bought expensive cedar,

cypress and sandalwood for fine cabinetry.

But his favorite part by far came when a piece had been completed to Jacob's satisfaction. His father would first examine the object up and down, in and out, checking every joint, dowel and rail. Was it flush? Was it square? Was it plumb? Was it balanced? Was it elegant? If it was all these things, he would smile deeply and say the magical words, ***"Mark it!"***

Then, in an almost weightless delight, Joseph would take the heavy iron bearing the brand of Jacob, Master Carpenter of the House of David the King, and place it in the glowing coals of the shop hearth. It seemed to take forever for the tip to become the radiant red it needed to be ... but once it was, Joseph would lift it with reverence and a look of utmost concentration. Now he needed the strength and steady hands that God had given him.

He paused for an instant over the spot to be marked, then pressed it to the wood. For a split second, it would seem to hesitate and dance giddily at the surface, much like the feeling one got from trying to push the northern poles of the astrologer's mysterious lode stones together. But then, with a rapidly curling ribbon of fragrant white smoke, it bit satisfyingly home ... and there it would be ... the maker's

Joseph would take the heavy iron ...
and place it in the glowing coals of the
shop hearth.

mark that would tell the world where the work had been born.

So excellent was the quality of Jacob's work that he was respected, admired and even envied in the craftsmen's quarter of Nazareth. Apart from his father's skill, there was something else that Joseph had begun to notice about him. All the other artisans and merchants did all they could to attract the custom of the nobles and the rich. A plum commission meant quite a bit of money and prestige. It would be foolish not to drop everything you were doing if a member of a great house should come to your shop, and that was the rule everyone obeyed. Everyone, that is, except Jacob. If a poor farmer should come to him first, that job would be completed to the utmost of Jacob's ability before he would start on anything else. No exceptions, no favoritism of any kind.

The rich, accustomed to special treatment, had not learned the virtue of patience. Jacob lost many golden opportunities because of his principles, and one of the effects was a family purse that had little in it for luxuries. Oh, there was always food on the table, a fire in the hearth and clothes on everyone's back ... but Joseph had only the white homespun his mother had woven to wear to the temple, and the boys of the other artisans in the quarter had fine Sabbath robes in a rainbow of colors and designs.

*... until the fight was over, and then
he was released to pick up his
beaten friend.*

Joseph had reached the age where it mattered to him how he looked. With the pack instinct for cruelty, the other boys would finger the hem of Joseph's plain robe and say, *"What splendid cloth! Your father must be a great carpenter indeed to be able to buy his son such a rich robe!"* They were always quickly rewarded with the fight they had sought.

Shem always tried to help Joseph defend himself against the gang, but there was no sport in the single blow it would have taken to eliminate him. Shem's little reed-thin arms were effortlessly held until the fight was over, and then he was released to pick up his beaten friend. It always puzzled Shem why Joseph should care at all about what any of those boys said. There was certainly nothing to fine cloth, so far as he could see. The goldsmith's little son was always dressed in cloth far richer than any of theirs ... not because of his father's affection, but because it was how Ruben felt a son of his house should be seen. Joseph was robed in his father's love, and Shem couldn't think of any raiment finer than that.

One day, Jacob spotted Joseph in the midst of one of those fights. As the master carpenter approached them the gang split up and fled down several narrow alleyways. Jacob demanded of Joseph the reason for the fight. Joseph's shame, added to his anger, embarrassment and the unwritten code of honor that has always existed between boys, forbade him to speak. Shem, always at Joseph's side and ever mindful of his feelings, also said nothing.

Several days later, as Jacob and his son were hard at work on a table for the dowry of a poor farmer's marriageable daughter, a richly-robed servant from one of the most noble houses in Galilee entered the shop. The servant inquired, *"Are you Jacob, the carpenter?"*

"I am," Jacob replied.

"My master," said the servant, *"has need of a carpenter at once. His new stallion has kicked down his stall and it must be replaced by a stronger one. Will you come, please?"*

"I'm sorry," said Jacob, **"but I have work here that must be finished first. It will be at least two days before I can attend to your master's barn."**

"But my master will certainly make it well worth your while. Come, man, he won't wait a single day, let alone two."

"Then you must go and find someone else."

"Wait!" Joseph suddenly cried. **"Papa, I can finish this table. I'm sure I can. Please – go with this man."**

"Joseph – "

"Please, Papa. I'll be careful ... and you can check my

work tonight and if I've done anything wrong, I'll do it over again."

"Joseph, you'll go back to your work now without another word." Jacob turned toward the servant who was standing by the entryway and said, **"I'm sorry you were delayed. My answer is still the same. Peace be with you."**

"And with you," said the servant, who looked wonderingly at Jacob for a moment, and then left.

Except for the sounds of the iron rasps on wood, the shop was ominously silent ... a silence that seemed to explode in Joseph's ears. Finally, he could bear it no longer and he blurted out, **"Papa, why – "**

"Joseph, I know what you're going to ask," Jacob replied before the question was out of Joseph's mouth. **"It's as I've always told you. One job must be completed before a new one is begun."**

"But Papa, ... I know I can finish this job myself ... and with the extra money you would have made, I ... "

"You what?"

"Nothing."

"You what, Joseph?"

"It ... it's just that all the other carpenters, smiths and merchants do special things for the rich and get paid well for it. Why can't you?"

"Joseph, what other tradesmen do or don't do isn't my concern. How this shop is run IS my concern, and what you are suggesting is wrong."

"But WHY is it wrong, Papa?"

"You really don't understand, do you, Joseph?"

"No, Papa. No, I don't understand at all."

Joseph felt the warm weight of Jacob's big hand on his shoulder. *"Well, one day I'm sure you will."*

Jacob and Joseph returned to their work. Two days later, Joseph put the maker's mark on the poor farmer's table.

The next three years saw many tables, chairs, plows, ox-carts, doors and chests come out of the shop of Jacob and his son. By the time he was seventeen, Joseph was taller than his father and stronger than any two men in the merchants' quarter. He was no longer provoked into fighting by the other boys. A single look from him was sure to silence any whispered words on the way to and from the temple.

The stronger Joseph became, however, the more he began to notice a growing weakness in his father. Try though Jacob

did to ignore and deny it, he was becoming the prisoner of a rapidly-increasing and painful swelling in his joints. As the months passed, Joseph found himself having to do more and more of the work until, at eighteen, he was virtually in charge of the shop.

Jacob still struggled in when he could on the crutches Joseph had made for him, but now it was to Joseph that the customers brought their requests and paid their money, and it was Joseph who spent each day but the Sabbath laboring in the shop, from the first blush of dawn until the purple of the evening.

In the midst of all this, Joseph had been surprised – and delighted – by the betrothal and marriage of Shem to Miriam, a sweet dumpling of a girl with high color and buoyant spirits. Not since they were little boys playing caravan bandits in the hills had Joseph seen his friend so happy. When an overjoyed Shem ran to Joseph one day to tell him that Miriam was with child, Joseph began to steal small parcels of precious time to fashion them a cradle … and what a cradle!

For the bed, Joseph selected the purest cedar from Lebanon for its beauty and fragrance. For the rails and rockers, he found the stoutest Judean hardwood. He balanced it with infinite care and burnished and buffed it to a mirror-

For the first time, he applied it ... and with all the love in his heart and all the skill at his command.

smooth gloss. The final touch was the most important of all. Especially for this occasion, Joseph had commissioned Micah, the blacksmith, to fashion him a maker's mark iron of his very own. For the first time, he applied it … and with all the love in his heart and all the skill at his command.

Joseph presented the cradle to Shem and Miriam, who accepted it with astonished gratitude. When their little son, Aaron, was born, the cradle became a great comfort. It held the infant with the tenderness and strength of an oriole's pendant nest. No hatchling was more secure than little Aaron, no mother happier than Miriam, and no father prouder than Shem. His tiny chest visibly swelled in the presence of his family, and even Ruben (impressed that his frail-looking son had fathered such a robust heir to his house) began to treat Shem with a measure of respect.

Like the selfless person that God had made him to be, Shem wanted only to share his happiness and good fortune with his friend. He'd sneak away from the goldsmithy whenever he could and regale Joseph with stories about his courtship, about Miriam and, most importantly, about the new and fascinating things his baby son had done. Sooner or later, though, Shem would get around to the inevitable suggestion:

"Joseph?"

"Yes, Shem?"

"Joseph, do you know what?"

"No. What?"

"You should get married, Joseph."

"Should I?"

"Yes, you should."

"I see."

"And do you know why, Joseph?"

"Why?"

"Because ... oh, I see. You're making fun of me. Alright, Joseph. Go ahead. Work yourself into an early grave! See if I care! Be lonely! See if I say one word!"

Silence.

"Joseph?"

"Yes, Shem?"

"Joseph, guess what the baby did today!"

In his heart, Joseph knew that Shem had a point. After all, he was eighteen, and as such he'd be rather an old bridegroom now. There was certainly no virtue in waiting from that standpoint. But where to begin? What to do? All his time was taken by work. If he were to keep the shop going, that

couldn't change. No – the only possible solution would be to hire an assistant so that he could go about the necessary and time-consuming business of matchmaking, courtship, betrothal and, finally, marriage.

The prospects of finding proper help, however, gave Joseph far greater pause than the prospects of finding a wife. As an established tradesman, Joseph would be a prize catch. He would certainly have his pick in that regard … but an assistant! One who would be skilled, dependable and – above all – honest … that would be difficult; perhaps impossible.

Joseph's fears proved to be all too true. Once the word got out that the shop of Jacob and Son was in search of an assistant, Joseph was besieged by dozens of boys and men, each one more unqualified than the last. There were beggars, cutpurses and drunkards. There were lunatics and runaways. As much as his heart went out to some of them, there was no one with even the most basic of the required skills. To stop the sad procession, Joseph allowed himself a rare lie. He sent out word in the marketplace that the position had been filled. Within a week, the inquiries had stopped.

Shem, desperate to be of help, volunteered to be Joseph's assistant for as long as it took and in spite of Ruben's bullying objections … but the toughness of the wood and the weight of

The "boy" dropped the axe and turned
around to face Joseph.
"My name is Mary."

the tools proved too much for his tiny, valiant frame. It took all of Joseph's creativity and humor to ease the agony of frustration that tortured Shem in his inability to do this great favor for his friend.

Work was a balm as well as a curse in the days that followed. It distracted Joseph from his troubles while at the same time being, in a way, the cause of them.

One day, while on the road to the grove where he collected raw timber, he saw something that made him stop in his tracks. He watched a boy in the distance – perhaps he was fourteen or fifteen – splitting fence rails with a double-bitted axe, then shaping and joining them … but with a confidence and expertise that Joseph could only see as great talent. Joseph tied his donkey to a bush at the side of the road and began to run across the field to the boy. Who was he? Might his father allow him to work at the shop? Could this be the answer he'd been praying for? Joseph reached the boy just as he was sinking the axe deeply into a sturdy log. With a sound like the crack of a cattle whip, it fell neatly in two. **"Well done!"** Joseph exclaimed. **"Well done, indeed. Tell me, boy, what's your name?"**

The "boy" dropped the axe and turned around to face Joseph. **"My name is Mary."**

The months that followed saw one of the happiest (if most unusual) courtships that had ever been seen in the village of Nazareth. Mary worked side by side with Joseph every chance she had, and Joseph delighted in her company and in the relaxed, confident way she bent to the heaviest of tasks. It didn't diminish her femininity at all ... her manner was such that she impressed without raising critical eyebrows. She seemed so natural in this work.

Jacob loved Mary instantly, as did his entire family. She had the gift of putting people at ease by simply being herself. She accepted others without reservation, and people seemed to be at their best in her company. Even the difficult Ruben found it possible to laugh at himself when she was around. As for Shem ... well, if it was possible for anyone to be happier about the turn of events than Joseph and Mary themselves, it was Shem. He and Miriam entertained the engaged couple at every opportunity. It was a time of laughter, rejoicing and excitement about a future that seemed to brim with good hope.

And so it was a great shock to Joseph's family and friends when all at once, without warning, he became silent, moody and withdrawn. They were further mystified by Mary's sudden disappearance. All Joseph would say is that she had gone to

visit her aunt. When asked when she would return, he'd only snap, **"I don't know,"** and bury himself in his work.

Joseph's mother, Leah, tried to explain the whole situation away to Jacob. With all his physical pain, he didn't need yet another burden. *"He's a bridegroom-to-be,"* she would say with false brightness. *"He's only nervous, Jacob. Try to remember how it was for you."* Jacob knew his son too well to be fooled so easily. There certainly was something else, but Joseph avoided his father and refused to speak about what was bothering him.

The worst shock for Jacob came when he learned that Joseph had begun turning poorer customers away in favor of richer ones. Not only that ... the quality of work for the poor (once Joseph got around to it) was careless and slap-dash. The maker's mark iron stayed on its hook, cold and unused. No matter what was troubling him, Joseph couldn't bear to put the maker's mark to work that didn't deserve it.

Jacob called Joseph before him and demanded to know why his principles were being violated. Jacob looked into the face of his grown son. He saw his innocent baby boy, his happy toddler, his puzzled, willful teenager and the strong, handsome young stranger he had become all at once.

"Father," Joseph said tightly in reply, **"It's time this**

The maker's mark iron stayed on its hook, cold and unused.

business was run like a business. I'm tired of working my life away for nothing."

"*Joseph!*" Jacob exclaimed, "*Do you even hear yourself? The shop has always given us everything we've ever needed. And it will do the same for your son and his son.*"

"*My son,*" said Joseph, "*should I ever have one, will not be dressed in homespun rags.*"

Shem didn't need to be asked for his help. At first, Joseph tried to tell Shem yet again that nothing was wrong. The harder Joseph tried to change the subject, however, the more adamant Shem became. Finally, unable to bear it anymore, Joseph turned fiercely on his friend and shouted, "**This is none of your business, anyway! Get out! Get out and don't come back!**"

Shaken as he was, Shem held his ground. "*You'll have to throw me out, Joseph. That's the only way I'm going to leave.*" Pushed to the limit of his endurance, Joseph grabbed his friend by the cloak as he had grabbed his boyhood tormentors years before. He pulled violently and felt the rich material tear in his hand. The sound of it hit Joseph like a thunderbolt, and he fell to the floor in deep, wracking sobs. Then, he felt a hand on his shoulder. He looked up and saw, as if for the first time, the clear, fearless face of his best friend.

"Whatever it is, Joseph," Shem said evenly, *"I stand with you and I'll never desert you."*

"It's Mary!" Joseph cried at last. **"She's ... she's ..."**

"Is she with child, Joseph?"

"Yes."

"Oh, my dear friend ... you've put yourself and everyone else through all this torture, and for what? Maybe the gossips will have a little something extra to chew on, but that's nothing. Why, this kind of thing happens all the time. You know that."

"Shem ... "

"Let's go to your parents now and put their minds at ease."

"Shem! You don't understand!"

"But I do, Joseph! It's like the righteous man you are to blow this out of all proportion ... "

"Shem! It isn't mine!"

A flood of terrifying images crashed in upon Shem. Joseph and Mary were betrothed ... and even in easy-going Galilee, where piety was relaxed, Mary was guilty of adultery. The penalty – if Joseph accused her, which he was bound by law and tradition to do – was death. Shem knew how deeply and

thoroughly Joseph loved Mary. It was the same as the way he loved his Miriam, and he knew that the pain Joseph was in had to be intolerable.

This would go beyond the gossips. Nothing could stop it. The House of Jacob might be scandalized; perhaps hounded out of business. As Shem struggled with all these thoughts, he couldn't bring himself to accept Mary's having done such a thing. Shem and Miriam knew Mary and loved her like a sister ... but Joseph would never lie about this ... no! It all wasn't possible! And yet ...

On top of all this was the urgency of time. Soon would come the days of the census! The dreadful Roman census! As an heir of his line, Joseph would have to travel to the City of David to be enrolled ... and if he were to take Mary as his wife and if the child were male, he must be enrolled too, or face "the extreme penalty of the Law," as it said on the leather decree posted in the village square. What that meant exactly was open to question, but bitter experience had taught them that caution was best where Rome was concerned.

As for Herod, the King – everyone knew that he was a mad dog and capable of anything. He passed up no opportunity to brutalize his subjects for the benefit of his Roman masters, and they rewarded his excesses handsomely. The question of

Mary would have to be handled quickly ... and all the options ended in despair in Joseph's care-worn mind.

Shem said nothing. What he wanted to express to Joseph knew no words. He looked again at Joseph ... his eyes reddened by weeping and lack of sleep. Shem put his small arm around Joseph's shoulders as they sat on the dusty floor of the shop. Shem began to hum a song they used to sing together when they were little boys. Joseph began to hum along, and in a few moments, he fell into an exhausted sleep.

Shem stayed close by his friend all that night, denying himself sleep in case Joseph should waken suddenly and need him. Several times Joseph cried out in his sleep. It sounded, at first, as if he were fighting with someone ... but after a time, the sounds took on a different character. It seemed as if he was almost laughing.

When Joseph awoke the next morning, the first thing his eyes focussed upon was Shem – who was looking disheveled, distressed and very, very serious. Just like that, Joseph began to laugh.

"Joseph, what are you doing?" Shem asked. The laughter began to build.

"Joseph," said Shem in a tone of growing annoyance, *"I'd like to know what's so funny."* This sent Joseph into whoops

of laughter punctuated by high-pitched hiccups.

"Joseph!" Shem insisted, *"I'd like to know what's so funny. Here I spend the whole night in this shop, and ..."* By this time, Joseph was completely incapable of speech. He was in the grip of that awful, wonderful, belly-cramping laughter that God reserves for special occasions. In spite of himself, Shem began to laugh along. Soon, the two of them were holding their sides and laughing the way they had on that unforgettable day when the Rabbi had to put them both out of class. Finally, after minutes that seemed like hours, the storm of laughter had spent itself.

"Oh, Shem, did you stay here all night?"

"Yes, I did. You don't have to thank me."

"Thank you."

"You're welcome. Now, I've been thinking, and I've come up with a plan that I'm sure will work – "

"Yes, I'm sure it will, but I don't need a plan. Everything's all right."

"What?"

"Everything's all right. I know what to do."

"What? What are you going to do? Something crazy? Please don't do anything crazy."

*Soon, the two of them were holding
their sides and laughing ...*

"Calm down. I'm not going to do anything crazy."

"Then what are you going to do?"

"I'm going to marry my betrothed and prepare for the birth of my son."

"YOUR son?"

"That's right."

"But you said … Joseph, you're not playing some terrible trick on me, are you?"

"Of course not."

"Joseph, God forbid that one or both of us has lost his reason, but you told me just last night that this child wasn't – "

"Shem – "

"Don't interrupt me, Joseph Ben Jacob! Wasn't yours."

"Well, he is mine, you see."

"No, I don't see. I don't see at all. Has some miracle occurred since last night?"

"Yes."

"What?"

"Yes. Just as you said. A miracle has occurred."

"Joseph, I'm tired. I'm not thinking clearly and I have to go home and go to sleep for a long time."

*Their words were few and clumsy, as
each tried to make the experience
bearable for the other.*

"It certainly sounds like you're thinking clearly. That's just what you should do."

"Good night, Joseph."

"Good night, Shem."

The flurry of activity in the days and weeks that followed made everyone feel rushed and constantly breathless. All at once, it was time for Joseph and Mary to set out for Bethlehem, the City of David. The goodbyes were anxious and painful. Mary was very near her time, and the last thing she needed was days of jouncing up and down on the back of a donkey.

Joseph was already tired out, owing to sleepless nights spent in finishing the plum commissions he had won. He hadn't spoken to Jacob all during this time. He knew how his father felt about the new approach to business he was taking, but for heaven's sake! The world always made stern demands, and now there was the child and this latest Roman tax … money was the only answer, and why Jacob couldn't see it that way was a vexing wonder to his son.

Joseph had been dreading saying goodbye to Jacob, and his heart pounded as he went into the lamplit room where his father lay. Their words were few and clumsy, as each tried to make the experience bearable for the other. Whatever their differences, whatever pain they may have caused each other, they were father and son. All the cedars of Lebanon, all the silks of Asia and all the taxes of Rome couldn't change that. Their parting was imperfect, but their connection had survived.

As Joseph and Mary moved toward the thoroughfare that would take them to the caravan trail out of Nazareth, they became aware of a soft, bell-like sound coming from the pack on the donkey's side. They stopped and Joseph fished around in the burlap for a moment. He withdrew a beautiful golden goblet to which a note was attached. *"Dear Friends,"* it read. *"This is the first article from my father's shop that bears my own mark. Don't get swelled heads because it's not for you. It's for your son. Don't let the Romans see it! May God always be with you. I love you — Shem."*

The journey was a hard one – sweltering days, frigid nights, the constant grit of sand and dust, short rations and, above all, the ever-present fear that the child would be born far away from shelter and help of any kind.

When Bethlehem finally came into view, Joseph and Mary felt the first rush of relief they had known in days. They joined the thickening crowd of weary people at the city's gate. A Roman centurion and several guards were inspecting people's

belongings before they could enter the city. It seemed that anything of value was being taken. Joseph tried to think of some way to hide the golden goblet with Shem's mark before it could be grabbed from them, but greedy eyes were everywhere, and Mary's discomfort was rapidly growing in the long line. Better to draw as little attention as possible.

When at last they approached the head of the line, Mary was beginning to groan in pain. Just as the hands of the guards were reaching for the burlap pack, the centurion in charge waved them on through. The guards – just frightened boys themselves, really, far from home – let them pass. Joseph thanked the centurion. The tall man in the Roman uniform was just about his own age. Perhaps he had a wife and child himself, many hundreds of miles away.

Joseph and Mary made their way through the crowded lanes of Bethlehem. Joseph, distracted by Mary's growing distress, tried desperately to remember directions in the town he hadn't visited since he was a very young boy. Were the inns this way? That way? Was a potter's shop there before? Had it all changed or was it that he simply couldn't remember?

Mary's groans of pain were becoming more intense, and the jostling of humanity – all seeming to be moving in the opposite direction – was agonizing to her. Some faces were laughing, some set in anger, and countless others displayed an infinite variety of moods and expressions – but none afforded Joseph and Mary anything more than a sidelong glance before they pushed on their way. The sun had sunk below the western horizon and the world was growing darker and fainter.

Joseph was near panic as he just by chance caught sight of an inn. In the yard, an overworked steward was carrying huge buckets of water. Upon seeing the couple, he dropped his burden and ran to them.

"Please," Joseph said, **"My wife is very near her time. I must get her inside."**

"Yes – yes ..." said the steward, looking anxiously left and right, *"only – oh, let – let me help you."*

Joseph and the steward lifted Mary off the donkey's back. Despite the cold evening wind, she was drenched with sweat. The steward fumbled for the door and slowly, they entered the inn.

Servants were scurrying to and fro among the milling tenants. It was almost the same as it had been in the teeming streets. The innkeeper caught sight of the steward and shouted, **"What are you doing? Why are you bringing these people in? You know we have no more room!"**

"But – you can see, sir … she's about to have a child."

"And you're about to lose your job."

"Please," Joseph interrupted, "Please help us. My wife can't have the child in the streets. There must be something – anything."

"There is nothing," the innkeeper insisted. "The only roof I can offer you is the one over the stable."

A cry of pain escaped Mary's lips.

"All right," Joseph said, "show us where it is."

"Are you mad?" said the innkeeper. Ignoring him, Joseph said to the steward, "Please – take us to the stable."

They made their way through the company … through the din of the steaming kitchen and back out into the shocking cold of the night air. They crossed the moonlit cobbles to a sturdy-looking stable. As they entered, the warmth of the animals, all contented and eating hay, was comforting and reassuring. A sky light illumined a clean bed of straw, and Joseph and the steward laid Mary upon it as gently as they could.

"I'll see to your donkey," the steward said as he ran back into the night.

"Thank you so much," Joseph returned.

*As he placed the precious bundle softly
on the hay, a bright beam of light
shone upon them …*

At last, alone but for the animals, with cries of pain that turned to cries of joy, the little couple brought their son into the world. From their pack, Joseph took the cloth his mother had woven and wrapped it around the infant.

"Let me have him now," Mary said, weakly.

"In a moment," Joseph said. *"Let me help you get something to eat and drink."* Joseph looked to find a safe place to lay his son, and he saw a stout wooden manger filled with sweet, clean fodder. As he placed the precious bundle softly on the hay, a bright beam of light shone upon them ... and in that light Joseph saw something familiar as his own hand in this place he'd never been before. There, weathered and worn but unmistakable, he saw his father's maker's mark on the stiles of the manger – and, at last, he understood.

There, weathered and worn but
unmistakable, he saw his father's
maker's mark on the stiles of the manger
– and, at last, he understood.

Tom Hegg, author of the much-loved *A Cup of Christmas Tea*, is a writer, teacher, actor, husband and father. Trained for the classical repertory stage at Carnegie-Mellon University and the University of Minnesota, he spent five seasons with the Tyrone Guthrie Theatre in Minneapolis. While there, he played Charles Dickens in Barbara Field's adaptation of *A Christmas Carol*. It was then that his romance with writing began, and it's small wonder that the holiday season surfaces again and again in his work.

Tom teaches drama at Breck School these days, and still acts from time to time in and around the Twin Cities. *The Mark of the Maker* is his third collaboration with Warren Hanson, following *Up to the Lake*, their book about summers in northern Minnesota. The Heggs — Tom, Peggy and Adam — make their home in Eden Prairie, Minnesota.

Warren Hanson was born and raised in Yankton, South Dakota. After graduation from Augustana College in Sioux Falls with a degree in speech and drama, he and his wife Patty moved to St. Paul, Minnesota, where Warren attended the College of Associated Arts to get formal training in the one thing that he had loved since childhood — art. He has worked independently as an illustrator since 1974.

Warren uses both his talent in art and his background in theater to bring stories to life. He first listens carefully to Tom's oral reading of the text, letting each story tell him how the art should be done. His illustrations, type selection and book design become the actors, dramatizing the story on the page, rather than the stage.

Warren works in his home studio in St. Paul, where he lives with Patty and their children, Cody and Lacey.